Econo Parasites

By Harry Harmon

This is dedicated to all the young men and women who
are inheriting the mistakes of our past.

We now look to you to be the next leaders and producers
to salvage what's left of our Republic.

I've tried to expose those "Creatures of the State"
who are trying to control every aspect of your life.
Protect yourselves and take back
what is rightfully yours.

Best of Luck!

ISBN: 1-448-61928-9

EAN-13: 978-1-44861-928-3

Published in the United States

June 2009

Content

Introduction

Understanding economics requires no "exceptional" knowledge. There is no great mystery. Basic economics is not an art that requires special talent. It's not a science requiring years of study to comprehend. Economics, like gravity, is a fact of life! Economics affects everyone, everyday. All it takes is the comprehension of a few specific definitions and a little common sense.

If you do not have an understanding of basic economics, you are at a huge disadvantage to the economic Vampires, Parasites and Cannibals who will misuse this knowledge to suck the economic life out of you. Governments and leaders may change but the methods used to control the people and their production, have remained the same throughout history.

As we proceed, you will note that there are no references to books or experts. No additional study is required. This is an intellectual exercise between us. Additional research sources are provided at the end but are purely optional.

Economics requires just one simple math formula.

Production minus Consumption equals Capital

Pr – Cm = Cp

That's it! Every aspect of economics derives from this simple formula. Every activity of CIVILIZATION will fit into one of these 3 categories. I kid you not! So, if all of economics is this simple, why are there so many different ideas and opinions on the subject? Why is there so much confusion?

Could it be the misinterpretation of these basic economic concepts causing the problems? And let's not ignore the possibility that the mystification of such an important subject gives power to those who would want to keep us confused and in the dark (as you will see shortly).

Let's start with some simple definitions. You can look these words up in any dictionary but to keep this simple, I will give you my definitions and you can compare these with your own ideas or what others have to say.

Formula Definitions

Production (Pr):

Any improvement to a natural resource or existing product through labor or ingenuity to enhance its benefits to the individual (Micro-Economics) and to all of mankind (Macro-Economics)

Consumption (Cm):

The "using up" or depletion of any "Production" (including natural resources and labor)

Capital (Cp):

Any "Production" <u>not consumed</u> that can be used for future "Production" or "Consumption" for the benefit of the individual producers.

From this point, any reference to production (producers), consumption (consumers), or capital (wealth) pertains specifically to these definitions.

Our Economic Formula and Civilization

Ever since the first individuals took some rocks (natural resources) and created a number of edged, pointed tools, began domesticating the wild beasts and cultivating wild fruits and grains, economics has ruled the development of civilization. For our purposes, let's define civilization as simply **"The peaceful co-existence of a large number of individuals"**.

When production is only sufficient to provide for the basic consumption requirements of survival, meaning production and **most all potential capital is consumed**, civilizations remain small and isolated. As individuals use natural resources to create products, or more efficient ways of production, or new uses for existing production, in other words, production begins to exceed minimum survival consumption, civilizations grow and prosper.

Capital builds civilizations

Let's keep our economic example simply just to lay some ground-work. We will use our primitive individual making "tools" from raw materials. He makes a number of such tools. He keeps a few for himself and trades the others for berries, wild grains or maybe some pelts. He uses some tools himself (hunting, gathering, and planting) and also keeps some tools for later use.

Production: Tools.

Consumption: natural resources for tools, food, clothing.

Capital: extra tools that can be used or traded in the future.

His production benefits himself and others. Note that those who provided the berries, grains or pelts also enhanced natural resources by their own labor. Everyone involved in this economic transaction produced something from his labor and received a benefit from this exchange of goods.

From the people who created the first tools, to the people who cultivate our food, to those who build everything we produce today, all production should benefit the individual doing the actual producing and will definitely benefit the individuals who consume that production.

From this simple example, we can see two important points to understand.

1. One man's production can be another man's consumption.

2. All fair and legitimate <u>economic exchanges</u> are between two or more **Producers**, who each bring something of value to the exchange.

We can draw a corollary from this understanding:

All economic exchanges between Producers and Non-producers are either voluntary such as charity or involuntary through theft, fraud or coercion (the threat of force).

The basics of economics are simple enough for anyone to grasp. Is it too simple? Has the world we live in today become so complicated that our basic formula no longer applies?

Let's see.

Capitalism

All production <u>not consumed</u>, creates capital.

Again, let's use our common sense here. If Capital is the difference between what is produced and what is consumed (and it is), **then capitalism must be the determination of how capital is used.** If this is true, then everything pertaining to economics must also pertain to Capitalism. What other form of economics is there?

Socialism, Fascism, or Communism are not economic models, they are political ideologies using force against the producers to claim and redistribute their capital. One thing these ideologies have in common is their **extreme dislike of Free Market Capitalism,** *which is really a dislike of individual and economic freedom.* Why is that?

Could it be a power struggle between individual use of capital (freedom) and the "collective elite's" claim on our capital (servitude)?

Part of this struggle seems to be the common misdirection by certain people (politicians, academics and media shills) who blame our current deteriorating economic condition on Free Market Capitalism. **That's like blaming a perfectly good car for an accident** when it was the driver who let the car get out of control.

Again, since all future economic growth, beyond survival consumption, is determined by the use of capital, (consumption reduces capital and works against future prosperity) there must be more to this story of Capitalism.

You hear the term **"Free Market Capitalism"** degraded almost every day but how many times have you heard the term **"Controlled Market Capitalism"**. These two concepts are really based on who gets to say how capital is used.

In a free market, those who provide the production, and thereby the resulting capital, get to say how their capital is used. In a controlled market, someone other than the producers get to say how the capital is used; such as governments or other special interest groups using government force.

Let's take a moment here to talk about force. Much of our understanding of the use of force pertains to physical violence. However, force can take on many forms.

Here's an example: you are driving down the highway and all of a sudden a police car pulls up directly behind you. That little doubt in your belly, "did I do something wrong?" is coercive force. Now the police car pulls out, passes you and moves on. That relief you feel is the (temporary) removal of that potential use of force.

Maybe you can think of other examples such as an unexpected audit from the Internal Revenue Service.

The very threat of potential harm; loss of property; loss of freedom, is a form of control by the fear of force without actual physical force having been applied.

Free markets work by voluntary association. Controlled markets work by the **threat of force under the "Color of Law"** (defined as "the appearance or semblance, <u>without substance</u>, of legal right. Misuse of power, possessed by virtue of law made possible only because wrongdoer is clothed with authority of State"; *emphasis added*)

As long as we have a legalized money monopoly creating money out of thin air (more on this shortly) controlled by a Central Bank owned by private international bankers; The **Federal Reserve Bank (FRB)**, and as long as we have a government that spends trillions of our capital dollars on redistribution plans AS THEY SEE FIT (even against the will of the producers who created it, (that's us)), we have a **controlled market economy**.

Anyone who claims that free market capitalism is the cause of our economic problems (and therefore we need more regulations) either has a personal agenda or is simply **intellectually challenged**.

Capitalism does not succeed or fail, "it just is". It's only the creation or lack of creation of capital and its uses that succeeds or fails.

Any time someone other than the actual producer can dictate by force (in any way) the use of our production and capital, we no longer have free market capitalism.

The next time someone tries to tell you "our economic problems are the failure of capitalism and the free market"; I hope you now know better.

Profit and Loss

It seems like nothing creates more contention about economics than the pursuit of profits. Somehow, it must be immoral or a crime against society to seek to benefit from your own work and, heaven forbid, the work of others. But what is profit, where does profit actually come form?

Profit is the pursuit of "Capital" as defined in our basic formula. A more narrow definition would be the difference between the cost of production (raw material or parts, labor, administration and compliance) and the **Marketable Value** of the actual product produced.

I'm defining **marketable value** as the minimum exchange rate where a profit exists. Sell at or above the marketable value and you create capital; sell below marketable value and you reduce capital; sell too much below marketable value and you destroy potential capital.

Profit comes from the efficient use of our natural resources and labor thereby reducing their consumption. Enough inefficient use of these resources increases consumption and creates a "Loss". It is profit that allows for future production and growth beyond a simple primitive (survival) society. Losses waste resources, reduce future production and impoverish the individuals of a society.

If you condemn the profit motive, you are condemning capital; by condemning capital, you are condemning future production; by condemning future production, you are condemning CIVILIZATION!

Supply and Demand

The **Price** (or exchange rate) of a product is determined by thousands of voluntary individual actions based on product supply (availability) and demand (wants and needs).

When supply and demand are relatively equal, prices can be maintained near the products "marketable value" price range, generating sufficient profit to continue to produce and supply the product.

When demand exceeds supply then prices need to rise to attract more investment and enterprises into this particular manufacturing or service arena to build up production capabilities to meet the supply shortages.

When supply exceeds demand then prices need to fall to attract more customers to buy the product, building up more demand. The enterprise may need to adjust its resource costs like labor and overhead (lower wages and or job layoffs) to accommodate this lower price.

Of course, if lower prices do not increase demand, then the product may not be suitable to compete in the marketplace (demand is not sufficient to justify production). The resources and labor of these losing enterprises needs to be re-allocated to other uses.

Government forced price controls of any kind interfere in this process, giving false signals to producers resulting in mistaken allocation of resources and capital.

Employers versus Employees

In a free market, labor costs would be mutually set by the interaction of supply and demand between individual participants. Employers need employees and employees need meaningful work. Even labor unions and business owners could come to agreement on these costs as long as force was not part of the equation. In a controlled market, either the union or the business is given the "upper hand" by government regulations that endorse or condone the use of force by one against the other.

Side note: Are unions inherently Socialist in nature? Remember, Socialism is a political ideology using the force of government to control production. Collectives such as unions may be social (beneficial) by nature without being politically Socialistic. The difference is the use of force and the usurping of the power of government to their own ends.

In a nutshell, Social unions = Voluntary associations for a common cause without the use of force. Socialist unions = Voluntary or involuntary associations (like closed shops) using actual force or the implied force of government regulations to demand compliance with the union's wants.

Neither labor (unions) nor business has the right to use force to coerce the other to their will. Criminal acts by either side should be prosecuted and restitution made to the injured. Even if individuals have the right to work, which they do, they do not have the right to work for someone else without mutual approval of the terms of employment.

Economy of Scale

Many of us have been led to believe that big business is evil. Big business is just a bunch of greedy bastards. Well, not exactly.

Big Business versus Small

Like profit, business growth is the natural course in the pursuit of efficiency in preserving resources and creating capital. Big business, in and of itself, is neither good nor bad. It is only efficient (creating production and capital) or inefficient (destroying resources and potential capital).

After all, wasn't a major part of the **American Dream** to be able to start a small business and by filling the needs of our customers grow it into a successful big business? Big businesses, that produce products that meet the wants and needs of others, benefit society with their efficient use of natural resources and labor opportunities.

It is only when the force of government enters the equation that corruption, theft and private property rights are violated with the protection of our so-called laws and regulations.

Without all of these regulations would big business corruption and fraud go away? Of course not, but without the use of force and the protection of these government regulations, other smaller companies would be able to compete and take business and labor away from any company treating their customers or workers poorly.

The auto industry is a good example with the major US car companies unable to compete with the more efficient foreign companies; destroying so much potential capital that the government has to bail them out with billions of our taxpayer dollars.

But don't worry. I'm sure our government will soon make new laws and regulations that will deny these successful upstart car companies the ability to compete in our markets. Maybe the "Green Initiative" will be the tool to make it impossible to build cars in America without government subsidies and control.

Lobbies write most laws and regulations

Consider how all these regulation are instituted. Maybe you believe that our representatives write these regulations for our benefit. Think again! (In fact they rarely even read them.)

I remember reading that there are literally thousands of lobby groups in Washington DC. Even one is one too many as it implies our Congress can be manipulated (gee really?). The primary function of a lobby group is for their attorneys to prepare legislation favoring their particular industry or special interest group. These lobbyist are paid millions of dollars to cajole, intimidate and/or bribe our legislators with promises of campaign contributions and election support (or the threat of opposition).

Judging by who actually writes these regulations, it's a good bet it's not to benefit us. Just imagine if you could pay someone a few million dollars in order to control entry into your industry worth multi-billions; what a deal! We've got the best government money can buy!

Consumption

Consumption is probably the most misrepresented of the economic concepts. Consumption encompasses all expenditures from raw materials to parts and labor that reduce potential capital. For the individual, consumption can be characterized into some basic components.

Basic Consumption Components:

Tier 1: Food and Water, Shelter, Clothing, Energy, Medical, Protection and Safety.

Tier 2: Education, Transportation, Property, Recreation, Charity

Tier 3: Taxes, Interest, Inflation, Regulatory Compliance

Tier 1 components are universal. Your very survival may depend on them.

Tier 2 components are important but are usually optional. I'm sure you can come up with other expenditures that are important to you. Most of these expenses are voluntary most of the time at least to the extent that your very existence doesn't depend on them.

Tier 3 components are the greatest threat to individual capital and wealth accumulation (and personal liberty). In most cases, they are imposed by government force or financial fraud or both and trying to avoid them may bring about dire personal consequences from the State.

Business Consumption is only slightly different. For instance, you could replace food with raw materials or parts; shelter with office or factory, etc.

The purpose of any enterprise is the same as for any individual; produce more than you consume to create capital for future growth, stability and longevity.

Contrary to socialist propaganda, it is in the best interest of any legitimate enterprise to treat its employees well, protect its capital investors, and not infringe on the private property rights of others. This is true even if for no other reason than it is more time and cost effective and therefore in the best **self-interest** of the company managers and owners.

Without corporations usurping through political bribes (I mean contributions) and other influence, undue favorable treatment under government "regulations", true and fair competition would eliminate those enterprises that violate employee or private property rights in short order.

My purpose here is not to go into every little detail of each spending issue. Everyone knows (or should know) that whatever you produce whether from your labor or your ingenuity, has a limit (even though in some cases the rewards of creativity can be great, it still is not infinite).

The greater your consumption is in relation to your productivity, the greater the reduction in your potential capital and wealth. Don't forget to consider your debt obligations. Debt is a claim against your future productivity and capital. While borrowing may seem to side-step the basic facts of economics, at least temporarily, your production and capital will have to readjust eventually.

The only way an individual can even think about retiring (moving from full time producer to full time consumer) short of government subsidies, is to create, save and invest your capital wisely; an almost impossible task in today's controlled economy.

Just look at our limited savings possibilities with artificially controlled low interest rates basically forcing an individual into higher risk ventures.

Gone are the days when you could just put your savings in a real bank and earn enough interest to steadily build a retirement fund for your future.

Gone are the days when you could count on the buying power of your savings over time.

Gone are the days when one income was sufficient to support our families.

Let's put the blame where it belongs. **We can thank the Federal Reserve Bankers and our government "central planners" for corrupting our once free markets and destroying our economic prosperity.**

What is Money?

As civilization and the "division of labor" expanded, bartering became more cumbersome. So man invented **Money**! Without a proper understanding of money, trying to understand economics is a futile endeavor. Here are some questions for you to contemplate.

1. Are money and capital the same thing?
2. Are capital and wealth the same thing?
3. Can you create capital (or wealth) by simply printing more money?

Money (currency) is not the same as capital. Money is simply a <u>substitute medium of exchange</u>. In fact, 21st century money is predominately a digital transaction representing nothing more than credits against <u>potential</u> capital or wealth. This is another area where I think confusion rules the day. The fraudulent idea that a printing press or a digital entry can create wealth **can only be maintained <u>by believing that money itself is wealth</u>.**

While money can **represent** capital or wealth, that is not the same thing as **being** capital or wealth. This is particularly true when the money can be created out of thin air as the Federal Reserve System (FRS) with the participation and complicity of Congress has been doing to the tune of trillions of our production dollars.

Remember our simple formula. Capital is created (and can only be created) by consuming less production than is produced.

Where is the capital that validates our current fiat currency? ("Fiat Currency" is simply money made **legal tender by law**, in our case an (arguably unconstitutional) act of Congress).

What production value did the Federal Reserve Bankers or Congress create to justify this expenditure (and destruction) of our capital?

Future production and capital that we, the American producers, will now have to create and **surrender to them through currency debasement or taxation under the threat of force.** Where is our free market voluntary exchange of produced goods?

I think it's pretty clear that an **American "free market" no longer exists**.

And yes, the meaning of capital and wealth can be interchanged. However, I would take it a step further and say that wealth is the long-term capital not used to enhance near-term new production.

In other words, **wealth is capital in reserve**.

Economic Vampires

While vampires of horror stories may not be real; economic vampires certainly are. Folklore depicts vampires as the top of the food chain feeding on those poor humans who happen to cross their paths.

The elitist central planners in government, banking and the corporatist who use the force of government to confiscate our production and capital are greater real life blood-sucking vampires than anything from fiction.

My purpose here is not to go into great detail about Federal Reserve System machinations but to keep this simple. In a nutshell, here's how it works.

The Federal Reserve Bank (FRB), <u>a private corporation</u>, has been granted by Congress the legal monopoly to create money at will and either funnels it to Congress through budget and appropriation bills through the sale of "US Treasuries" or distributes the money to the FRS member banks (with or without government approval as the FRB is privately owned by international bankers).

Our current monetary system is theft on a grand scale. The ongoing bailouts of private banking, financial, insurance and manufacturing enterprises are good examples of their actions.

How much "new money" bailouts to its own banking system is unknown because the FRB is not subject to any "public audit". Or worse yet, how much of our currency has been funneled to other international banks to beef-up their US dollar reserves?

We don't know. The **"Federal Reserve Act"** actually prohibits any meaningful financial audits by Congress or even the Government Accounting Office, supposed to audit all government agencies.

A private banking cartel has been granted **"State Secrets"** status. Even Congress, which gave it license to exist, by law has no auditing authority. The FRB is even above "Freedom of Information Act" requirements. Why, because only government agencies are subject to the FOIA; again confirming that the FRB is a <u>privately owned</u> money cartel.

Deregulation

It's a total scam claiming that it was deregulation of the free market that caused our recent (ongoing) financial crisis. First: What free market? Second: Nothing gets deregulated without the approval of our elitist central planners.

The only thing that has been "deregulated" is the banking, finance, and big government-endorsed businesses run by the very vampires who are destroying our prosperity.

The only "deregulation" has been to allow the central bankers and their cohorts more government power and force to destroy competitors and suck-up their assets for pennies on the dollar.

But I digress! The issue here is that the banking system and the government get the use of this new fiat money first, not the people (the only true producers of capital).

Monetary Inflation

Suppose your neighbor were a master printer and could print money undetectable from the "real thing" (sic). You're looking to sell your house for $200K. A potential buyer says "I'll give you $190K". "Printing press man" says "I'll give you $210K". The potential buyer who really wants to buy your house increases his bid to $215K. "Printing press man" raises his bid to $250K.

You sell your home to the highest bidder; "Printing press man" prints the counterfeit money and "buys" your house.

Did he not just steal your property with his "non-production backed" counterfeit money? Did he not just steal the potential new home from Mr. Potential Buyer? Did he not just "spend" $250K of phony money into your neighborhood?

Could the potential buyer who is limited to the use of his own capital from his own production (or future capital through borrowing) ever outbid the unlimited supply of counterfeit money from "Printing press man"?

Notice also the attempt by you and the potential buyer to negotiate a **price** relative to your individual perceived values until "Printing press man" with his virtually unlimited funds enters the bidding, forcing the prices ever higher.

"Ah", you say "But I just received $50K more than I expected." Life is good! But suppose this counterfeiting has been continuing on a wide scale everywhere and you find that all houses that used to be in your price range now cost more (higher real estate prices based on counterfeit money). Your gain will likely only be temporary plus all other potential buyers are now affected by this flow of counterfeit money into your neighborhood.

Creating money out of thin air has the same effect on every product in the marketplace as it does here on houses (more phony money chasing limited real goods).

And, if it is ever found out that the money is counterfeit, it will be deemed worthless and will buy you nothing!

Now suppose government gave "Printing press man" the legal right to print as much money as he wants (by using force under the Color of Law). Does the government have the right to legalize an act that the individual would otherwise be punished for?

This is probably the most important question any civilized society can face!

If you believe that the "government collective" has the right to "legalize" criminal acts or the right to criminalize natural rights in order to license and control us (with protection payments to the State), <u>then you are the problem!</u>

I certainly hope not!

The Effects of Inflation

"Shave and a haircut: two bits". For you youngsters who probably never heard this little ditty, two bits equal 25 cents. For most of the first half of the history of the united States, barbers would give you a shave and a haircut for 25 cents or less. Today, you would be hard pressed to find a barber for $10.00. That's a minimum increase in cost of 40 times, just for a haircut. Why? **It must be the fault of those greedy barbers!**

Or maybe not! Maybe it's because barbers now have to have government licenses and special approved training as required by government regulation (to limit entry into this enterprise). Or maybe it's because our money supply has been expanded faster than real production can justify (more dollars chasing less goods). Or maybe it's both government intervention in the marketplace and the FRB currency expansion.

Rising prices are not the cause but the result of inflation. Not only can inflation be seen in rising prices, but also in the deterioration of quality and reduction in quantity of the products we buy. Economic enterprise is fighting a losing battle of cost reductions to keep prices down while the Federal Reserve Bankers create more non-capital-backed (bogus) money to throw our American enterprise "under the bus".

Inflation is the **intentional** debasement or counterfeiting of the individual's medium of exchange. It is no less a theft of production and property than when committed by "Printing press man"!

Bubbles and Busts

Bubbles:

Creating new money out of thin air gives the first users of this money (banks, government and their corporate and social partners) an unfair advantage against all real producers of capital (that's you). "Bubbles" are created by flooding the economy with currency (inflation) and credit (low interest rates) with no corresponding production or savings of capital to justify such currency expansion.

The part of the economy that gets inflated depends on which activities the government and central planners are currently subsidizing through tax, investment, and business regulations (like the Community Reinvestment Act, tax deductions and artificially low interest rates for mortgages did for home prices).

Busts:

The Federal Reserve Bank can burst a bubble by removing currency and credit from our economy (raising interest rates). The government can burst a bubble by changing or removing favorable "bubble activity" regulations.

But even our central planners can't force our economy beyond the capacity of what the actual working people can support or justify with their production and real capital (savings).

In an economy the size of the United States, it can take years, even decades, before our basic economic formula will burst a bubble. At some point, the bubble activity becomes saturated by the production activity trying to follow these false market signals (for instance, more houses and higher prices than the economy can support).

At some point, no matter how much money or credit the banks make available, the individual will no longer have the capacity to produce beyond his own consumption and debt load. He will no longer be able to create enough capital to support the higher and higher prices that the bubble demands. In other words, **he no longer has the economic capacity to carry all of this debt.**

Case in point: The rate of actual individual saving (real capital) has continued to go down over the years to nearly nothing. This means that real capital has been siphoned off from our economy by the actions of the government's taxes and regulations and the banker's counterfeit money.

It is only recently, in spite of our rulers' insistence that we spend, spend, spend, that the individual has finally realized (either consciously or not) that we had better start saving our capital for our future economic survival.

More Big Bubbles

State Government budget deficits are getting as much "out of control" as the federal budget. State governments, particularly the ones with large "vital services programs" (welfare) are just as much a destroyer of individual capital and wealth as the feds are. These government parasites have taxed their state's individual producers (the host) to near the point of economic death.

At some point, the federal government will have to bail out these states the same as they are doing for the banks and businesses "too big to fail". The shortfall of what government can continue to take in from the people already taxed and regulated to their productive limits will simply be provided by more fiat money creation.

The state deficit bubble will now be spread throughout the nation. Any state that has maintained a relatively efficient government will then be saddled with the debts of the more welfare-prone capital consuming states.

Even though the feds are claiming "no bailouts for the states" start looking for the bailouts (maybe under a different name or process) to begin with billions of new fiat dollars (this is in addition to the billions already distributed from our federal taxes each year). My opinion is that bailouts for California, New York and possibly some other states will start sometime soon.

Could these state bailouts be the final straw that breaks the nation's back? There are already a number of state congresses particularly in the south and northwest talking about secession for a number of other reasons. The bursting of this bubble could actually be the dissolution of the United States as we know it. We'll see.

The Federal Reserve Fiat Currency Bubble

Of course the "**Mother of All Bubbles**" is already well underway. With a nearly 12 trillion dollar national debt (all fiat money created out of thin air) that represents nearly the total annual production capacity of the whole country; a 3.5 trillion dollar national budget for 2010; a budget deficit this year approaching 2 trillion dollars, how much more debasement of the American dollar can our nation stand?

Not even the Romans had the capacity to inflate their currency with the precision and proficiency of our government and the Federal Reserve Bank. The Romans could only debase the quality of their metal coins until they were worthless as money; ending their reign as the ruler of the known civilized world. Without the ability to create paper or digital money, the Romans were amateurs at currency debasement.

The bursting of the dollar bubble will see the US dollar discarded as the world's reserve currency making America just another failed empire.

It is possible we could see hyperinflation just like every country that has followed this path from ancient Rome to Wiemar Germany, to Venezuela and Zimbabwe.

The goal of our elitist central planners is to replace the US dollar with a new world currency to expand their total control and theft of the world's production and labor. How did we get into this mess?

Theft of a Nation

How to steal the wealth of a nation:

Replace "Printing press man" with a government-endorsed private bank, the Federal Reserve Bank. Authorize it to print whatever money it needs whenever it wants without any ties to any legitimate capital or wealth created from actual production. Are not the banks which loan us this "non-production backed" paper currency stealing our property? But wait, there's more!

A common robber does less damage to us than the Federal Reserve Bank (FRB); at least he will only take what we have in our pocket. Let's consider the multiple robberies committed by the government sponsored Federal Reserve System.

Big Theft #1: The National Debt

The US Treasury creates debt instruments (bonds, treasuries) to raise money. The Treasury sells them to the FRB in exchange for new digital currency paid by simply crediting the government Treasury bank account for the purchase price of these debt instruments.

The government (they claim that's us) has to repay the FRB for this money, **plus interest**. Some FRB apologists argue that the central bankers give the interest back to the government, but so what! Even if this were true, it doesn't change the fact that the national debt of nearly 12 trillion dollars was still created with nothing more than digital entries in a bank ledger.

Here's a thought. Wouldn't it be less damaging to our nation if the US Treasury simply printed the money and spent it into the economy without creating debt or interest? Maybe this is not the best solution but it is still better than allowing international bankers to control our money supply (our very medium of exchange).

Big Theft #2: Theft of Our Property

The Federal Reserve System requires (allows) member banks to only maintain 10% of their "capital" in reserve for potential withdrawals. Notice the use of the term "capital" as if banks actually create capital. The only capital that banks actually have is the capital that we save from our production and deposit with them. By only maintaining a 10% reserve, banks can lend up to 9 times the actual capital we deposit (**fractional reserve banking**). All loans above our real capital deposits again are simply created by digital credits from the Federal Reserve Bank.

These banks then use this credit to lend us money to buy things (houses, cars, etc.). Do we really own our property or are we just allowed to use things until we can't afford them any longer? I think our current housing foreclosures answer that question.

Legitimate Free Market Banking

A truly free market bank would never be allowed to pretend to have more capital than they actually have, period. All personal or business loans and all mortgages would come from bank customers who agree to participate in these activities either directly or even indirectly with long term loans to the bank. A free market bank would be a facilitator of these transactions, receive fees and possibly part of the return on investment but they would be acting on behalf of the real producers of this capital. They would not be stealing our property with fraudulent non-existent (counterfeit) money.

Big Theft #3: Theft of our Future Production

All money created through our current Federal Reserve System, whether through government debt or private debt, requires the payment of interest, **while the money to pay the interest itself doesn't exist.**

For example, if the Federal Reserve Bank creates 1 billion dollars and lends it out with interest of 5%, where does the interest come from? When we try to pay back this debt plus interest for a total of 1 billion 50 million dollars, the extra money doesn't exist and must be created by the FRB, **again more inflation with more interest due and more theft of our production.**

So not only do the banks collateralize (claim of default ownership) this debt with our property, the interest must come from our future production. In other words, this is a system of perpetual debt. Perpetual debt means perpetual theft of our production.

This is a monetary system of indentured slavery!

Are You a Criminal?

Since 90% of all the money for every bank mortgage, car loan and credit card debt is created out of thin air with no real production or capital backing it (counterfeiting), have you become party to a crime? You are party to the theft of the property from the producers of whatever you buy. You are paying the home builder, car maker, computer company with "funny money". If this money had come from "Printing press man" and you willingly spend his counterfeit money into the economy; you are an accomplice to a major fraud, and that's a felony.

Don't worry though; your partners in crime are the government sponsored counterfeiters, so you won't be prosecuted. This government has made every American a criminal! Again, does the government have the right to make an illegal act, legal? Oh, and by the way, there is no honor among these thieves. You will have to pay them back, **with interest**, by producing real capital from your own labor and production or lose the property you rent (I mean buy).

Our so-called "national debt" represents a tremendous loss of potential economic security of every man, woman and child in America and for generations to come. **This plainly is theft of our future production and capital!**

It is a sad state of affairs when those who perpetuate this theft against the American people are treated with **undue respect and admiration**. Is our country a Constitutional Republic or an Aristocracy? Do the people who steal our wealth and destroy our capital deserve to be treated as royalty **or the thieves they really are**? You tell me!

A Gold-Backed Currency

There are many who would like to see our currency backed by gold and/or silver. There are plenty of good reasons for doing this on which I agree. However, even if our money were backed by gold and silver, this just proves my point. **Money is not wealth!**

Until money is actually exchanged for the gold and silver backing it (or something else of value created from production), the currency only represents potential wealth. **It is the gold and silver that is the actual wealth.** Why? Simply because these metals are enhanced natural resources (by mining, smelting and stamping) and are the production part of our economic formula. Any part of production not consumed is capital or wealth.

But doesn't our money (fiat currency) fit into our economic formula? It's the enhancement of raw material (paper and linen) and ingenuity (creative printing and security provisions). Isn't that Production? Yes it is.

So what is the difference between paper money and gold-backed money (or any other commodity-backed money)?

Value! The market itself determines what the relative value is by comparing supply (availability) and demand (wants and needs). The cost of production is much higher and availability more limited for gold than for paper money. In fact, the production of paper money is virtually limitless. And what is the limit on digital currency, which makes up most of today's money? None!

But here is the real difference. Federal Reserve Bank money is a direct claim against the property of every American. **"Full Faith and Credit of the United States"** means that the full productive capacity of the United States backs our currency. That's you and your property and production **enforced and collected by the Internal Revenue Service for the benefit of the bankers and our nation's creditors.**

A gold-backed currency would be a claim against the commodity itself. **A commodity-backed currency would free every American from this claim against our very livelihoods.** That, in and of itself, would be reason enough to change to a commodity-backed currency.

So I ask you? Which currency would you rather have? Or, the big question, why don't our government leaders want what is obviously best for us?

The Case against Gold and Silver

Many people, including our government leaders, scoff at the idea of going back to a **"Gold Standard"** as a form of sound money. Sound money meaning a dollar backed by something other than the current fiat money system. They claim that gold-backed money is old fashioned and has already been abandoned **because it didn't work.**

When they say, "It didn't work", what they really mean is they don't want a money system that curtails big government spending by imposing a limit on creating money that a commodity-backed system would entail.

Big government with all of its warfare, welfare, big business entitlements and subsidies depends on fiat money. It also depends on the ability to tax our labor and property (control us) as a re-payment and collateral structure for the debt that this fiat money creates.

The Case for Gold and Silver

Gold has been used as a medium of exchange for thousands of years so it has a pretty sound history for maintaining its usefulness as money. If this is true then why did the "old gold standard" fail?

When Congress instituted gold-backed paper currency instead of setting the weight (quantity) and quality of the gold backing the dollar unit, **they set the market price of gold itself.**

There is no constitutional authority to set market prices! Our original gold standard failed because it was based on a **controlled market strategy**. The "old gold standard" was never based on free market price action. Arbitrarily setting the value of gold at a price of $20 or $35 or even higher sets the currency up for (planned) failure.

When one country tries to control the price of any commodity (natural resource), while the rest of the world allows market conditions to set the price, inevitably a price anomaly will occur. When the world gold prices began to exceed the US controlled price, a "run" (redemption of paper money for our gold) by other countries took place. I believe this is what caused the Bretton Woods agreement to be discarded.

To add insult to injury, throughout the Bretton Woods era, American Citizens were prohibited by law from owning gold. The FRB, using the force and cover of government, confiscated all of our gold at $20.00 per ounce and then immediately raised the price to $35.00. Forget the Brinks gold robbery, this theft by our elitist rulers has got to be the greatest gold heist in history.

A gold-backed currency that simply states the quantity and quality of gold to be redeemed (say 1 gram of 24 carat gold) would allow the gold "price" to fluctuate in the open market without changing (actually protecting) the underlying purchasing power of the currency.

Private Commodity-Backed Money

There is also absolutely no reason why anyone couldn't create money who owned gold or silver (or any acceptable commodity), and was capable of proving and protecting the gold or silver backing their currency. **It doesn't need to be government controlled at all**.

Of course, the Federal Reserve Bankers won't have any of that. So they got their buddies (or pawns) in government to pass the **"Legal Tender Law"**. The bankers wrote this law for themselves so that they would be the only ones allowed "by law" to create money of any kind.

They have corrupted the very essence of any possible free market; our "medium of exchange". Our ability to make a legitimate value-exchange from producer to producer has been seized by a bunch of devious, elitist, non-producing Vampires!

Government(s)
Economic Parasites

What governments have that you and I do not have is the "assumption" that they have the legal right to the use of force.

The politicians, bureaucrats and all of their alphabet agencies who gain from the powers given them by the State under the **"Color of Law"** and who use these powers to live off of our individual production are parasites as dangerous as any health risk in nature. They will continue to infect our economy until they eventually kill the host.

It will take the "strong medicine" of an informed and vigilant citizenry (that's us) to bring this parasitic disease under control.

Question: "If using your own logic and common sense, you can agree with me that our simple economic formula is a basic fact of life; **"you can't create capital and wealth out of thin air"**, why do you believe (if you do) that governments have some kind of special power that allows it to circumvent this economic fact?

Is there some mystical function of macro-economics that leaves individuals subject to this economic limit while governments and large special interest groups are exempt?

Let me explain the reality of government in one paragraph. No government, not our local, state or federal government, not any other country's government, no government that has ever existed at any time in the history of the world has ever breathed one breath of air, had one thought or original idea or created one iota of wealth, ever!

Only individual can breathe, think, create and produce. Governments, corporations and all "collectives" are not living creatures; they have no life of their own; they are run by people. And people, even large groups of people (**even democratic majorities**) have no more power over the economic facts than you do.

The very idea that a "government body" can provide the individual with benefits that the individual can't provide for himself or with the cooperation of his neighbors is an absurdity based on the fear of government force.

But, in the words of "Lewis Black", "It's an illuuuusion!"

Earmarks versus a Blank Check

There has been a lot of debate lately about the "evils of earmarks". This is just another attempt to confuse the issues of government spending. An earmark is a **specific use of funds** in a Congressional spending bill.

Again, using your common sense, if our money is going to be spent, shouldn't it be **specifically identified** as to what it should be spent on? The alternative to earmarks is issuing a blank check to the bureaucrats to spend our money as they see fit (usually used against the producers).

All government expenditures should be earmarked at the time of voting the spending bill into existence. How many Congressional bills would be presented if every dollar was earmarked for everyone to see? Still too many, but even so, to not earmark is to hide the potential use of those funds from the people.

I have no doubt that government spending is out of control. The new budget just approved by Congress will spend 3.5 trillion dollars in 2010. This year's budget is expected to create well over a 1.5 trillion dollar deficit. In other words, they intend to create and spend more money in the next year than at any time in the history of our country.

Instead of condemning this out of control government spending spree, we are led (misled) to debate and decry "Earmarks"! Give me a break!

"Divide and Conquer" as a political tool

Divide the people into classes by race, gender, national origin, religion, capital, sexual nature or political parties; pit one against the other for government favor.

Differences among people exist and always will. But it is government force on one side or the other that works against peaceful resolution and the "Rule of Law". Limit the government's ability to use force to interfere in our personal and economic lives and the natural course of human endeavor proves people will find common ground to live in peace.

Stop being a political pawn!

Government Force
and the Destruction of Capital

Or the "Guns and Butter" Warfare / Welfare State

Government is a consumer of production and a destroyer of potential capital. From an economic standpoint, the idea that government adds to the wealth of a country just isn't true. At best it provides a service but even good service is still part of the Consumption component in our basic economic formula. Worse yet, it is mostly paid for by Tier 3 forced Consumption.

I recognize there may be some who believe we should rule the world and kill everyone who might become a future threat to us (Warfare). And some who believe we should provide a minimum income to everyone in the country (Welfare). But we must also recognize that these endeavors expend our capital. Any attempt to spend our way to prosperity without individual production to offset this consumption **spreads poverty, not prosperity**.

Measuring our economic prosperity:

Attempts to monitor our economy with measurements concocted and controlled by government agencies or Wall Street and academic elitists are nothing more than attempts to deceive the people.

The fact is that government is an expense (a consumer of production). To claim otherwise by including things like military and government consumption as if they add to our production in our **Gross National Product**, while not including many of the Tier 1 consumption necessities in the Consumer

Price Index, are clearly attempts to hide the true condition of our economy.

Case in point: current monthly unemployment figures (April 09) show a decrease in employment (lost jobs) of more than 500,000 jobs. This figure was reached by subtracting over 70,000 new government jobs as if these jobs add to our nation's production.

All government jobs are paid for by the taxpayer or by creating new (counterfeit) money, not by producing an actual product. Do we really need more overseers using the power and force of government to rule us, consuming more of our productive capital?

The greater the size and scope of government, the greater is the consumption of the individual's production and the destruction of our capital and potential wealth.

The government even lies about its own tax revenue. As more and more people are employed by government and paid by taxes from the individual producer's real production, government employees are then taxed as well. These taxes are then added to the government's claimed tax revenue. Do you see the fallacy here? All of the taxes from government employees are simply recycled from the actual taxes from real producers. How can that add to the actual revenue that government claims it can spend?

So what's the point of taxing government employees? Here we get another look at the true "dark heart" of government elitists planning. Government employees are people too. They have the same wants and needs as the rest of us.

Translation: they need to be controlled and what better way than the strong arm of the **Internal Revenue Service (IRS)**.

It's no coincident that the **IRS** was enacted into law the same year as the Federal Reserve System. The IRS is the collection arm of the Federal Reserve Bankers. The threat of an IRS audit and possible confiscation of property is a powerful force for keeping all Americans (even government employees) in line. This applies to all government employees even those elected to higher office.

Remember how some of the new administration's appointments to high office were attacked for not paying all of their taxes. I'm not condoning their tax mistakes (evasion), creatures of the State should pay their "fair share" too (whatever that means?)

But what a diversion to entertain the masses and at the same time **remind us that no one is safe from the IRS**, not even government officials and politicians.

The central planner elitist vampires have to keep the government parasites in line too.

Government: Best Case

A government which is limited to providing the Tier 1 consumption needs of **"Protection and Safety"** from foreign invasion (national level) or domestic violence (state and local level) is the least damaging (costly) to our individual capital and wealth.

The National government should adjudicate disputes between the states. National government costs should be paid for by their member states (as the original Constitution called for) and not by direct taxation of the individual's labor and capital.

States should raise their funds by tariffs and service fees or even lotteries. Tier 3 consumption of inflation should be eliminated by using sound money. Regulatory compliance should be extremely limited or better yet left to private organization similar to (non-force based) "Underwriter Laboratories".

And of course, the one basic thing all governments should do is honor their own charter of existence; their own Constitution. How do you rate our government on these issues?

My score: **Total absolute abject Failure.**

Democracy versus Republic
Mob Rule versus the Individual

Democracy! Democracy! Democracy! This is the chant we hear practically from birth. Like missionaries of old, we should spread the gospel of our Democracy to the poor and downtrodden around the world. **If we have to kill a few innocent people in order to spread our "goodness", well, don't the ends justify the means?**

Someone once said that the bigger the lie; the easier it is to perpetuate. Spreading the "Good of Democracy" is such an outrageous lie that many, even those intelligent enough to know better, have come to believe this without question.

I'm not positive who said this, but I think it was Benjamin Franklin (or maybe one of those other original British terrorist) who said: "Democracy is two wolves and a sheep voting on what's for dinner". "A Republic is a well armed sheep".

A Republic is a nation based on the rule of law; while a Democracy is a nation based on the rule of men (majority rule over individual rights).

The truth is that the united States of America was formed as a **Republic** with a Constitution and a Bill of Rights to protect the people and bind the government to the "Rule of Law".

Those who swear an oath to uphold the rule of law that these documents represent and then disregard their oath are liars and criminals. Does this mean that we are being ruled by liars and criminals? In a word **YES!**

The reasons violators of these laws are not held accountable for their crimes are not so obvious. I blame it on the indoctrination of the American people by those seeking power and gain at the expense of all individual producers. Only by promoting Democracy can our rulers confiscate our property through unconstitutional taxes and "funny money" creation with the apparent <u>approval of the masses</u>.

Democracy is an abomination of majority rule over individual property rights and economic freedom. Democracy gives the elitist central planners the <u>force of opinion</u> of the misinformed, bribed and lied to majority, over the individual.

We are a Constitutional Republic with a <u>d</u>emocratic election process, not a <u>D</u>emocracy.

The sooner the American people can grasp the difference, the sooner we can return our country to the "Rule of Law" under a "Constitution" and "Bill of Rights" protecting our individual lives, property and production <u>from government</u> as our Founders originally intended.

The Paradox of Majority Rule

Another problem with a Democracy is the "Paradox of Majority Rule". It seems the assumption that the majority actually does rule in a Democracy is in itself a lie. Democracies are ruled by special interest groups with the majority mislead and misdirected by the controlled mass media into following the "collective group".

The "great majority" has no time for politics. They are too busy trying to survive. Add in the fact that most national candidates from both the right and left are already bought and paid for by the special interest groups who really control our voting choices. The "great majority" sees little hope or reason to "get involved".

Real individual producers are too busy producing; too busy trying to take care of their families; trying to meet their Tier 1 consumption needs and hoping to add a few Tier 2 wants as well. While all the Tier 3 "forced consumption" takes more and more of their potential capital and wealth literally destroying the "great majority's" economic power.

Not too recently the "great majority" was being told that it's their greed that caused the housing bubble. It's their "give me mine, now" mentality that is causing our financial problems. Now that the "great majority" is pulling back on spending and trying to save (get their financial houses in order), they are condemned for not spending enough.

What arrogance by the very elitist vampires and parasites who live off the production that the "great majority" produces!

Party Politics

The purpose of political parties is to divide and conquer the "great majority" on seemingly important issues. These issues are made to seem important by the special interest groups on both sides of an issue with the complicity of the corporatist controlled media (the **Tokyo Rose** of our day) while the elitist central planners wield the real control over our government.

Forget about the potential (or actual) electronic voter fraud. Forget about the actual scam that we have a real choice in who we can vote for. **Political parties and the deception that voting somehow makes our government subject to the people's will is the biggest con of all.**

Both Republicans and Democrats (third parties are minimized by voting rules written by the elitists) are controlled by the special interest groups who all want to use the force of government for their own agendas. **The goal of "party politics" is to grow the size and power of government in the direction of a particular ideology.**

Once in office, both liberals and conservatives compromise (Bi-partisanship, another hoax against the people) in order to get what they really want; more political power!

Politicians who consistently refer to our country as a Democracy are either stupid or liars, or worse!

Democracy is the illusion (or delusion) of government by the "will of the people".

A Republic under the Rule of Law

The original concept of a Republic brought into being by our Founding Fathers was one of the greatest events for individual economic freedom in the history of the world. **Too bad it has been corrupted by the ideologies of Fascism and Socialism <u>under the guise of Democracy</u>.**

Did you know that originally (before it was amended) the United States Constitution called for two Senators to be appointed by each of their respective States as direct representatives to the national government? It wasn't long until the power elite realized **it would be much easier to control our US Senators, if they had to "Win" election by popular vote.**

Today our US Senators have to appease the elitist central planners for admittance to one of the two major political parties to receive corporate or special interest backed contributions in order to compete for election.

No longer a position of appointment of merit by their fellow State representative (saving huge amounts of our wasted capital), they now must appease the populace more or less misled and misdirected by the corporatist controlled media to "get elected".

Honorable men and women, the very ones we need to represent us, are repelled from running for public office by the back-stabbing party politics, leaving us with the worst of humanity, **those who want or even need to have power over others.**

Too harsh? Maybe, but there are very few in politics today who don't fit this description! So, if I'm wrong, then Mr. Politician:

Honor your oath of office!!!

In a true Republic, no man is above the law. Every one of our politicians swears an oath to uphold and defend the US Constitutions which includes the "Bill of Rights".

Political parties and their corporate and special interest group sponsors would not have the power to corrupt our representatives, if our representatives actually lived up to this oath. Lobbies, both corporate and "special interest" (who write most of the legislation passed into law for the benefit of their clients) would all be out of work.

I know this for a fact. We have an actual "real life" example of how an honest man (one who honors his oath of office) can shut down these political connivers.

US Congressman Ron Paul of Texas has no lobbyist lining up at his congressional door. They know it is a waste of time as he would throw them out on their ears. Of course Dr. Paul (a real MD as opposed to a PhD in political science or other such parasite training) is too much of a gentleman to physically throw them out. *I just added that for effect.*

Side Note: in Dr Paul's congressional office he has a sticker on one of his in-boxes that reads:

"Don't steal, the government hates competition."
How's that for telling it like it is?

The point is, it's the current state of our national democratic voting system that corrupts all but the truly patriotic "stout of heart" such as Dr. Paul.

Maybe it takes representatives who actually have real lives as individual producers (who did not use the force of government to get ahead) with a productive life to go back to after politics.

Instead we have these life-time career politicians who become entrenched in their positions, passing new laws and regulation in the thousands of pages every year to rule over our lives like royalty.

As long as they don't upset the inner circle of central planners or the political special interest groups, these people continue to get elected no matter how corrupt or inept they may be.

Don't you think if we actually held our representatives to their oath of office (the law of the land), they might think twice about breaking those laws?

Until we stop thinking of politicians as somehow better than the rest of us (above the law), and start making them accountable to the "Rule of Law", we are doomed to be ruled by the political class of parasites we have today (with very few exceptions).

Courts against "The Rule of Law"

The Federal Supreme Court

The Supreme Court was established under the Constitution for one purpose and one purpose only. They are our last bastion of hope to determine the constitutional or unconstitutional aspects of the cases and laws that come before them. That's it!

They are not to set aside contracts, taking one's production in favor of another, unless a contract violates an individual's constitutional rights. (I'm not talking about the unalienable rights of mankind here, **just their own Constitution and the "Bill of Rights"** which is their duty and responsibility to uphold. It's their reason for being created in the first place.)

They are not to over-ride State's rights, except on constitutional grounds **to protect the individual from State abuse.** They are not to "make law" (that's Congress' job); but only weigh the constitutionality of those cases and laws before them.

The "Separations of Powers" concept depends on each branch abiding by the Constitution and each holding the other to the Rule of Law. The Supreme Count was to keep States, Congress and the Executive branch from violating our individual rights as described in the "Bill of Rights".

The appointment of Supreme Court Justices should be based on one criterion alone. Does he or she have a record of adjudicating cases by the Rule of Constitutional Law? **Their "life experience" and liberal or conservative ideologies are irrelevant in a Republic under the Rule of Law.**

Our courts need to either follow their own "law of the land" or we should amend or discard the Constitution so we can stop pretending "we are ruled by law and not by man's whims".

I know it is presumptuous for me to say that our Founding Fathers made some mistakes. However, some obvious mistakes have already been corrected by amendments (and some amendments over-turned their original good intent). But to me, the biggest mistake isn't even in the Constitution.

In the "Declaration of Independence", they stated that it is "self evident that all men are created equal". Sounds good, but it gives Socialism and Egalitarianism its foothold! It would be a sad world if we were all the same. It is our differences that make us unique and valuable. We are big and small, fast and slow, genius and average, rich and poor, leaders and followers.

The only equality we can and should actually protect is that "<u>we are all equal under the law</u>".

Who would adjudicate political crimes?

Of course, in order to have a judicial system willing to judge government crimes against the people, you must first remove the personal income tax. Before the laws were changed, all judges were exempt from the personal income tax. Should we resent their special privilege? No, we should resent the income tax itself but as long as there is such a tax, why should judges be exempt?

Here's the answer in one statement! If you, Judge, do not do the government's bidding, you will be subjected to the humiliation and possible property confiscation and loss of your position by an **IRS investigation and audit**. Need I say more?

Economics and Jury Nullification

No doubt, one of the most important functions of the Citizens of a free country is serving as jurors in the trials of our fellow Citizens (while we still have trials). More important than the "election vote", the vote of a jury is the greatest protection of our individual rights to our life, property and "**Production**".

Judges will try to tell you they are the authority on the law and you are only capable of judging the facts of the case. This is a deliberate attempt to confuse the public of the true intent of "trial by jury". **Juries have every right to judge the validity of the law itself; otherwise we are nothing more than government puppets.**

True patriots should never "skip" jury duty. It is one of our best chances to **take the teeth out of unjust laws** and capital confiscation.

Let's cut to the chase, how do you recognize an unjust law? First, a crime is any act of force or fraud against another human being causing a loss of life, property, or production? Second, stop thinking of "collectives" such as society or government as living beings. They are not. By the very definition of a crime, the State or "society" can never be the victim of crime only individuals can be victims.

Any law or regulation where no individual human being has been damaged is nothing more than capital confiscation for the benefit of the State. Use your power as a juror to Nullify them!

National Elections

How to cut the cost of elections and the economic waste that goes with them!

Every four years, we are treated to the spectacle of a Presidential election. This last election process spent (wasted) over a billion dollars of our hard earned production and capital. And for what; so we could fool ourselves into believing we actually have a say in who rules us at the national level.

Here's a free market idea; why don't we treat our federal government like a business. Why don't we let our "Board of Directors" (Congress) appoint the national President and VP like any corporation would appoint its own Chief Executive Officers?

The President would still have a four-year term, however, and here's the big difference in a Republic where no one is above the law. If the President violates his "Oath of Office", Congress (like any good Board of Directors) would be able to vote to remove and replace him with a new appointment. If the offense is grievous enough (like getting our young men and women killed in undeclared wars), charge him; give him a fair trail and when (I mean if) found guilty put him in jail.

Now I realize there are constitutionalists out there who might say that this would breach the "Separation of Powers" doctrine of the three branches of government (like that still exists) by making the President's veto powers null and void for fear of removal by Congress.

Even though I think the Executive Branch has way too much power with all of its executive orders (approaching dictator status thanks to a weak and complacent Congress) and needs to be knocked down a peg or two. That's not the point. Under the rule of law, disagreements of policy would not be a removable offense. Only violating the "law of the land" would be.

In fact, a President who did not veto an unconstitutional bill would be in violation of his oath. That would kind of turn things upside down wouldn't it? A President who actually protected Americans by vetoing unconstitutional bills? **Wow, what a concept!**

Let's also get rid of the national Senator elections. Let's go back to the original Constitution and have the Senators appointed from among their already elected State Senators by their respective State Board Of Directors (State Congress). Again, if they violate their oath of office, charge them; give them a fair trail and if found guilty, remove, replace and if justified jail them as well.

Why do we need State Congressmen <u>and</u> Federal Congressmen? The Constitution says that the national "congress should meet <u>no less than once a year</u> or in case of national emergency". **Obviously, our Founders didn't intend for this to be a full-time job!**

Why not just send the States' own Congressmen and Senators themselves as our representatives to Washington? Do we really need to have elections for both?

Look at all the money we could save and all the "political mischief" we could eliminate.

By having each state congress select its own representatives to the national government from within their own ranks, the individual, who would still be voting locally to elect their state representatives, would no longer be involved in politics at the national level.

Of course for this to work, we would be responsible for holding our state representatives to their oath of office, which is something we don't seem to do very well. But who knows, maybe with fewer politicians to deal with, we could do a better job of picking our representatives.

Oh, and give our state representatives an extra $100.00 raise and see how much time they spend in Washington passing national laws that effect (confiscate property and punish) everyone in America.

I know eliminating national elections sounds pretty radical, so let me explain my reasoning in the next chapter under **State Sovereignty**.

State Sovereignty

As each state is foreign to every other state, all states are foreign to Washington, District of Columbia. This goes to the very heart of state sovereignty. Texas and Florida and Pennsylvania and Montana etc, are all independent land designations (states) with their own governments.

These States make up the union of States called the United States of America, **making us American Citizens**; not the UNITED STATES OF AMERICA, a corporate entity making us U.S. (corporate) citizens of Washington DC (a subject for another day).

For instance, each state has its own driver's license, business registrations, taxes, etc. When you physically move from one state to another (or have a business formed in a different state), you must register your change of residency to the new state. So it follows then that the Citizens of each of these states are foreign to the Citizens of every other state and therefore are foreign to Washington D.C.

In fact, until the national Congress passed the Federal Reserve Act and the Internal Revenue Act, and the 14th and 16th amendments to the Constitution, we were all state Sovereign Citizens and Americans, not "US citizen subjects" of the federal government and their IRS.

Do we vote for the President of France or the Parliament of Britain? No! Do we vote for the state congress in the other states or just in the state where we live? So why should we, as state Citizens, be voting for a government that is foreign to us in Washington D.C.?

States do not need to secede from the union.

By getting rid of the onerous Democratic mob rule from our national elections and having the states appoint their representatives to the national government from their own elected Congressmen and Senators, states would regain their individual state sovereignty.

He who controls the flow of our money controls the nation! Instead of money flowing from the top down, giving control to Washington D.C., it would flow from the bottom up giving the power back to the states where it was intended by our Founders.

Taxation without legitimate Representation

Which is worse, taxation without representation or taxation with representation by incompetent and/or corrupt politicians? Not much of a choice is it?

Again the cost of the national government should be the responsibility of the states. Would that mean we would no longer be subject to the Federal Income Tax? **Would you be willing to give up national elections to get back your state Citizenship non-federal taxpayer status as an American?**

As state Citizens and Americans instead of US citizens (of D.C.), we would be foreign to Federal jurisdiction and would no longer be a "person(s)" subject to the IRS income tax.

How would that affect your capital and wealth potential?

Isn't that something worth thinking about?

Tier 3 Consumption

I have no doubt that the greatest drain on our economy and the greatest affront to our freedom is the Tier 3 forced consumption items of **taxes, interest, inflation, and regulatory compliance**.

When a government uses force to tax individual labor or capital production, it is claiming ownership of your production and your very being. It is claiming that you have no right to property or privacy without government approval. Taxing your labor and production by force is nothing less than legalized theft. (Even IRS agents are now authorized to carry guns as the "government enforcers" they are.)

It seems to me that most people can't even envision the possibility that we could provide the services we need for ourselves by voluntary contract and payment without a huge government bureaucracy hovering over us to force us to "be good". The ideal of true freedom has been "educated", "beaten" and "bribed" out of too many of us.

In a truly free market economy, government would be small and unobtrusive from the individual's prospective. If you have been paying attention, you can see we are a far cry from such a benevolent and non-intrusive low cost government in America. What we have instead is a **"mixed fascist socialist government leviathan"** controlling every aspect of our lives and production.

Controlled Market Capitalism

The opposite of "free market capitalism" is not fascism or socialism; it is "controlled market capitalism". Fascism and Socialism, (yes even Democracy) are the ideological tools used to establish a controlled economy.

A simple definition of fascism is the partnership of corporate and political elitists controlling the force of government for their own benefit. This includes the Federal Reserve Bank and its members and the military / energy / pharmaceutical / agricultural / media / industrial complex. By buying Congressional support through political contributions or by threatening to "ruin" political futures, wealthy corporatist gain control of the government agencies that are supposed to regulate their activities.

They use these regulations to control market entry and prevent any real competition to their market control. Their overall purpose is to redistribute our capital to the moneyed elite. Example: The FRB itself, Goldman Sachs, Citigroup, etc.

My definition of socialism is the usurpation of the force of government to claim ownership of production by "special interest groups" for the redistribution of wealth to those whom the central elitists want to subsidize or control.

They use many of the same tactics as the corporatist to gain government power. These special interest groups also buy political support from the masses (voters) by distributing to them a portion of this **"redistribution of wealth"**.

Some of this redistribution is to the special interest groups themselves. Example: $8.5 billion to ACORN who helped get the current President elected.

What these political ideologies have in common is the intent to grow a huge government bureaucracy for more control and redistribution of the wealth of our nation.

The answer is not more regulations that give these vile government elitist creatures control over our economy and our productive lives, but to eliminate their control altogether.

The government is about to give the UAW a major ownership position in the auto industry with the very large redistribution of the capital of its stock and bondholders to the union (read union leaders and their political cohorts). There is also legislation to remove private balloting for unionization votes so the union leaders can know how everyone is voting. I don't suppose that will lead to any intimidation of those who vote NO to unionize, will it!

Can anyone doubt that this is simply "payment" for UAW (and ACORN) political support?

Remember, government is a fiction. They are just people. We are perfectly capable of regulating ourselves through our local, county and state peace officers, a voluntary state and national militia or National Guard under individual state control (with probably a full time Air Force and Navy (and Marines) to man our national <u>defense</u> systems) and our local, state, national and even international courts to settle personal and business disputes.

There is absolutely no reason why these services and activities could not be provided by free market competition and voluntary consent. If you do not believe a free people are capable of self regulation, that only "governments" can "keep the peace", then you have a pretty low opinion of real economic freedom. But guess what! It doesn't matter. **Economics will rule the day!**

All Coercive Governments Fail in the end.

The use of government force by elitist central planners to steal the capital and wealth of a people has been the scourge of every civilization. Have you ever wondered why all the great civilizations of the past fall apart and disappear; well you are living those reasons today! You'd think by now we would know better.

Our simple economic formula explains it all.

Government consumes production. The greater the degree of government consumption is the greater the destruction of individual capital and wealth. The greater the destruction of capital, the poorer the civilization becomes. Finally there is insufficient capital left for future production and the civilization collapses upon itself.

As in all of history, the Individuals, the true producers, will reorganize and move on.

Maybe next time we can get it right.

Do Wars Benefit Our Economy?

Our intent here is to understand war from an economic standpoint. I'm sure most of us would agree that war is probably not the best use of our natural resources or our human endeavors. It should be noted however that we have been engaged in war (undeclared by Congress as required by their Constitution) on several fronts for nearly a decade and that's just the current conflicts. How is that working out for us economically?

My economic definition of **"War" is "the intentional destruction of property, production, and producers (that's human beings) on a large scale".**

We are told by our rulers that it was our enormous production of "weapons of war" during WWII that saved our economy and ended the Great Depression of the 1930s.

It was our massive military employment that eliminated the high unemployment rates of the depression. Even if that were true, how do you calculate the enormous lost potential production and capital creation of so many individual lives that wars have cost our civilization throughout history?

Let's use our basic economic formula and look at how war impacts our economy.

Production:

No doubt production would be high. A huge amount of natural resources would be enhanced by labor and ingenuity into new products for the benefit of the individual and all of mankind.

Well, I suppose we could argue that war benefits the individual and mankind by saving freedom and democracy from potential world dictators. Or just maybe wars are initiated by governments for the benefit of the "Elitist Central Planners" at the expense of the individual producers even to the point of death. Just saying!

With so much concentration on war production, other (peaceful) domestic production such as cars, refrigerators, washing machines, etc. are all but eliminated. You might even recognize this as a "War Bubble", (see Bubbles and Busts above).

In wars, price and wage controls and rationing are put in place, limiting individual domestic production and free markets even more.

Consumption:

Tier 1 expenditures: We could argue that the use of this production was for Protection and Safety. Of course, it probably didn't do a lot of good for the economy of those on the receiving end of these "expenditures", but then that's war.

Bombs and munitions, once used are destroyed, natural resources used up. Airplanes, tanks, and warships, all war apparatus damaged or destroyed are left behind. In some cases even perfectly good material is just discarded rather than go to the cost of bringing it back.

Tier 2 expenditures are all but eliminated (so much for our "creature comforts").

Tier 3 expenditures dominate the economy to pay for the war. Government control of production and property are at all time highs and consume huge amounts of our potential capital.

Capital:

Munitions, airplanes, tanks and warship not destroyed could be considered capital, but for whom. It belongs to the State. I don't think private individuals are allowed to use them.

We could claim the capital of the State is the same as the capital of the people. We could claim that, but it would be another lie. Remember, government does not produce or create capital; it only consumes (destroys) it.

We currently have over 700 military bases in 130 countries with an ongoing capital expense of about one trillion dollars per year, every year! Just think what we could do with that capital here at home.

War is the central planner's greatest weapon for the confiscation of individual production for the benefit of the State.

How can anyone in their right mind think that somehow the destruction of production, capital, property and lives could end the Great Depression? It was the bursting of the war bubble and a return to individual production for peaceful purposes; the reduction of government's hold on our natural resources including labor and the reduction in taxation of our capital that ended the Great Depression. It's just common sense!

Wars, Wars and more Wars:

The primary weapon of government control is not guns or bombs; it is fear. Fear is perpetuated by war!

So we have the war on terror, the war on drugs, the war on poverty, the war on disease, the war on education, the war on guns (coming soon) and even the war on capitalism itself (called wealth redistribution).

The one thing all these wars have in common is that the government central planners are conducting an undeclared (and undisclosed) war on the people and the individual producers of this nation.

Wealth redistribution is a government claim that the wealth of a nation belongs to the State and not to the individual producers. These are all government ploys for the confiscation and destruction of individual capital and production.

A country that constantly engages in war will eventually have to confiscate and squander its own citizens' production, capital and lives until it brings about its own financial destruction.

A nation of poor non-producing individuals, dependent on the State for survival, is a poor nation indeed.

Service Industries versus Manufacturing

Every man's production can be another man's consumption. In other words, some production depends on another's production to exist.

Service industries depend on manufacturing industries to survive. While services are important to our well-being and even our survival and those who provide services are valued producers; without a manufacturing base producing actual product, where will the production and capital to consume these services come from?

Again, using our own common sense, let's define our meanings of these industries as they pertain to our economic formula.

Manufacturing Industries are any part of "Production" that results in a finished product; such as food, medicines, cars, washing machines, air conditioners, furniture, computers and even bigger items like homes and factories, etc. or even parts for other products such as tires, motors, wiring, tubing, conductors, fabrics, bricks, cement, etc.

Services Industries are any part of "Production" that results in "Consumption" by another producer to maintain, protect, repair, beautify or in any way enhance the producer's efficiency or comfort such as computer technicians, barbers, food servers, salespeople, lawn care, truckers, military, and yes even lawyers and politicians (who are supposed to serve their constituents.).

Let's use our original example of manufacturing tools.

As more tools are needed, our toolmaker **teaches** employees to help in production. Another individual sees that someone needs to maintain the tools, so he becomes a tool sharpener; another sees the need for food service to feed these workers, so he opens a cafeteria.

You can see from this simple example that all service industries are of necessity supported by manufacturing endeavors. **Without products, what would we service?** Without producers of manufactured products, where would the original production or capital come from to pay for these services?

The farther we are removed from actual product manufacturing the greater the consumption of "services" affects our potential capital and wealth. If this is true, where does our capital go?

Here's your crash course in international trade. As our manufacturing of products moves to other countries, those countries begin to capture our future capital and wealth.

That's how China has amassed more than a trillion dollars of our capital. They then use this capital to buy our government treasuries becoming our creditor. They also consume our services making us even more dependent on their manufacturing and good graces.

At this rate, some kid in China calling tech support for his computer will be complaining about how hard it is to understand "that foreign American accent and their lousy Chinese"; and "why are these people stealing our jobs".

Why are we losing our manufacturing jobs?

Our manufacturing enterprises move off shore for one simple reason; it's more cost effective to do so. It consumes less business resources and therefore less capital and potential wealth.

Could there be other reasons or is it just their selfish greed for profits? Or, could it be that the use of government force through regulations, government support for labor unions, heavy taxation and unfavorable international trade agreements has something to do with our manufacturing jobs going away. What do you think?

Public Labor versus Private Labor

As our current unemployment grows, particularly the losses from what's left of our manufacturing jobs, government is expanding the public workforce. Is this a good use of our labor pool? Does this increase our production and capital wealth? Hardly!

Private labor is paid for out of production. Public labor is paid for out of taxes or newly created fiat money. Government is consuming from the same production that private labor is paid from. **There is no net gain in production.**

What you're not supposed to know is that all government jobs, all public work projects, **all government subsidized labor is consumption paid for out of our individual production.**

Government Employment

To report unemployment numbers by subtracting newly created government jobs is an intentional deception. Where is the production that these new government employees are creating? I suppose if you want to count more bureaucratic intrusion into our lives and more control over our production, then the government is doing a great job. However, I have a slightly different view.

Government employment gains more power for the "elitist central planners" by making more people directly dependent on government. The more private labor is moved to public labor the bigger the drain on the capital and wealth of our nation and the greater the loss of our own individual capital and economic freedom.

Public Works

Were the building of the pyramids and monument of antiquity a good use of natural resources and manpower or were they simply for the aggrandizement of the rulers?

But, you say, don't "public works" create production that benefits society? Don't roads and bridges and public building like libraries, museums or even federal buildings count as production? Aren't the individuals who do this work, producers? Yes, to all of this.

However, why do we need a middle-man (government) to redirect this work force? Why should we let the central planners tell us where the roads, bridges and buildings are to be built? Shouldn't that be a function of the marketplace to decide where something is needed, what is needed, and what isn't (maybe there wouldn't be any more infamous "bridges to nowhere")?

Why give up the power to control our production to those who would gain from it without producing anything themselves (parasitic politicians and bureaucrats)?

Public works is a political tool to gain power.

And never forget, all of these projects are paid for with our capital through taxes and currency inflation. All government action belongs in the Service Industries category; a huge rapidly growing "Consumption" of the capital and wealth of our nation!

War as a "Public Works" program

We need to keep reminding ourselves that government is a fiction. It is just another "collective". It is not a living being. No government has ever pulled a single trigger or dropped a single bomb.

As in all collectives there is an "inner circle" of people who give orders, set direction and (try to) control the members. Its supposed purpose is to benefit the members (usually at the expense of non-members). In reality, it is the inner circle vampires and their political parasites that gain the most benefit from the use of force.

Domestic and foreign wars provide the reason for more government employment of armed members to follow orders from their "leaders". We can believe that the purpose of these armed men is protection and safety but **the end product of war is always death and destruction.**

Contrary to what some believe, war is not the natural state of society. It is the natural state of the collectives' leaders who use force to gain or maintain power and capture natural resources and production at the expense of others.

To all you armed agents of the State, if the time comes when your leaders demand that you exercise deadly force to "contain" your fellow Citizens, **will you pull the trigger or will you honor your oath to defend the Constitution and the Bill of Rights and defend your fellow Americans?**

Economic Cannibals

Those individuals and special interest groups, who use the force of government as an excuse to become non-producers and live off the production of others by participating in the government wealth redistribution scams, are cannibals eating the substance of their fellow citizen's production.

Mad Cow Disease

Whose idea was it to take herbivores (plant eaters) and decide it would be smart to feed these animals the remnants of their own kind, turning cows into cannibals.

Welfare leads to the equivalent of **political mad cow disease**. Our elitist central planners have no problem feeding the substance of our production to others. They claim it's for the sake of fairness and equality as they gain more political power and control over the masses.

If someone came to your door and with the threat of force said, "Give me your money or I will hurt you". Wouldn't that be a criminal act? When the government comes to your door and with the threat of force says, "Give me your money or I will hurt you". Why is that not a crime? Can the government make a criminal act legal on the pretense that it is "doing good" for someone else at your expense? It's just plain theft.

Charity does not come from the threat of force or the barrel of a gun.

Welfare versus Charity

The government must really like poor people as it is intent on creating so many more of them.

I realize that calling welfare a "cannibalizing of our productive citizens" is a pretty strong and politically incorrect statement to make. So, I will soften this indictment of welfare recipients (not welfare) by stating that I do believe in helping those who need it. I also believe that welfare is just as much a trap for those who have less opportunity as it is for those who have to pay for it.

However, I have no such compassion for the corporatist or special interest groups who use the force of government to appropriate our capital and wealth. As creating money out of thin air is counterfeiting money; **welfare is counterfeiting charity** and for the same reasons. Control; control over those who receive welfare and control over the producers forced to pay for it.

Welfare is just another political tool.

Again, do we really need the government creating more bureaucracy that uses its power for more control over the people; particularly when there are legitimate charitable organizations that are perfectly capable of helping people (and have a history of doing so) without using force?

While Charity is listed as one of our **Tier 2 Consumption** items, there is no Consumption listing for "Welfare"; because welfare is not a function of economics. Welfare is a function of taxation and government wealth redistribution.

The Damage to the Individual in a Welfare State:

When we give help to someone directly or through a charitable organization, we feel good about helping. We don't give more than we can afford. We don't deprive our own families of necessities. We give voluntarily with goodwill in our hearts.

However, when society, by the use of government force, demands not only that we give but how much, even if it takes away from our own family's needs, then we have every right to feel resentment for the loss of control over our own lives. Unfortunately, this resentment may be directed at those receiving this help as well. Welfare creates and divides us into classes and pits one against the other.

When we receive help directly from family and friends or through a charitable organization, while we may not feel great about our current situation, we are certainly grateful for the help.

But again, when government force is used, disconnecting the act of charity from the receipt of this help, **it appears that the government is the giver and not the individual taxpayer.** Over time, this creates a sense of entitlement. After all, "it's the government's money and it's their job to take care of me".

Forced social welfare separates the humanity and goodwill in the act of giving from the act of receiving and alienates the true giver from the receiver.

Forced social welfare divides Americans to the benefit of those politicians, central bankers and other elitists in control of our government.

By building a society of individuals, either fearful of government confiscation or dependent on government for their very survival, power and capital is removed from the individual in favor of those in positions of government control of these processes and funds.

Fatherless Children

I've heard many people decry how the poor abuse welfare; how they don't take responsibility for their own care; how poor men "father children" and then abandon them. Could it be that welfare is one of the biggest reasons for this problem? It's probably right up there with the "War on Drugs"?

When the government tells a woman she can only receive welfare to feed her children when there is no man in the house, the father, **unable to earn enough to compete with the government's welfare,** is marginalized and moves (or is pushed) aside.

While social welfare may seem like a good idea, it is an ever-expanding trap working against the very people it purports to help. Long term welfare programs, unlike charity, become the "expected entitlement" and work against a person's sense of self and personal control and are detrimental to the well being of us all.

Welfare and Unemployment Payments

It is politically incorrect to ever criticize paying someone for not working. After all everyone needs help once in a while. The real question is how did we ever survive before government programs came along to rescue us?

Charities, churches, friends, family, neighborhood social clubs and even unions used to take care of people when they needed it. **And they didn't use the threat of force to take what wasn't theirs to give to someone else.**

The difference between then and now is "expectation". Once you formalize and regulate these payments, you make it a competition between the value of being productive and of not being productive.

You can blame the individual if you want to but when you compare the value of working against not working and the difference is negligible, it is only common sense not to work. In other words, **if we pay for non-production, we will get more non-production.**

The liberal minded have a genuine concern for the less fortunate. I don't question that. But you can't condone the use of force to turn money over to the government on the grounds that it is to help the poor.

Government is not about charity; it is about control and power. The sooner we recognize this, the sooner we will quit giving our power for individual prosperity and charity over to an abusive and out of control State.

How to Really Help the Poor

How do we help the poor without destroying the "middle class" and the individual producers? How do we help the poor without resorting to the use of force against others?

Return to a "sound money system" that stops the hidden inflation tax that destroys our dollar's buying power to keep Tier 1 necessities and Tier 2 'creature comforts" more affordable.

Remove international trade agreements that do not favor our own citizens and sends our manufacturing jobs "offshore".

Eliminate government regulations that give the big business corporatist an unfair advantage by instituting costly government compliance (red tape) that only they can afford. Stop overburdening small business and start-ups so they can create real productive jobs in their local communities.

End the "War on Drugs" that criminalizes addiction and drives social, emotional and medical problems "into the streets". This also affects the poor and minorities more disproportionately than it does most others.

End the "world empire building" that sucks nearly one trillion dollars a year from our production and puts our young men and women in harms way; again a disproportionate number of poor and minorities put at risk.

Is it possible that our rulers actually want to keep people poor to provide "cannon fodder" for their military industrial complex? I shudder at the thought!

Eliminate a forced confiscation of property and capital (federal income taxes), **depriving us of our right and <u>ability</u> to be charitable.**

This may not be everything we could do in a society (a Republic) where all individual are **treated equally under the law** but it's a good start to ending the ever-growing poverty in our country.

International Welfare versus Charity

When every year the United States government gives billions of our taxpayer dollars to other countries like Israel, Saudi Arabia, Georgia (x-Russia) Pakistan even Iran and so many more we don't even know about, these funds go directly to that government's political and military leaders.

Maybe you believe that this money is to help raise the people's standard of living (or even promote democracy) in our name. Think again. These funds are used to support military and economic control over their populations. These funds are used for the same government initiatives in those countries as our government uses here. Control of the people!

When we donate (give freely) money to private organizations like the "(International) Red Cross" or the many other charities with worldwide initiatives, that money, food and support goes directly to the people who need it most. It does not go to line the pockets of their parasitic government elitists.

If we really want to help other people in the world, government is not the answer. Their agenda is always more government and more control.

Imagine what the Red Cross could do with just a portion of all the billions of dollars wasted on all those other government parasites.

It's time we stop giving the power of our capital and production to those who would use it to the detriment of our fellow human beings. It is time to put an end to the destruction of <u>their</u> potential production, prosperity and capital **as well as our own.**

Social Security

There is an important message to be learned from the Social Security System: **The government cannot be trusted with our nation's wealth!**

The Social Security System is absolute proof that the federal government is a thief, a liar and a fraud. It makes Bernie Madoff look like an amateur in comparison. Madoff's self confessed money scheme has squandered 50 to 60 billion dollars of other people's capital while the federal government's Social Security System has **stolen trillions of dollars** <u>taken by force</u> from every individual producer in our country for more than 60 years.

I first got my Social Security number in 1962 while in high school and working part time as a busboy in a local restaurant. I remember well the pride I felt when I received my card in the mail with all the information that came with it (yes I was a product of our public schools).

Like a "rite of passage", I felt the power of earning my own way as an individual producer. (I still lived at home but at least it was a start towards independence). I tell you this so you know this information is not "hearsay". I have first hand knowledge of the lies told to me about Social Security from my youth.

Lie #1:

Social Security is a <u>voluntary</u> <u>private</u> *government protected* <u>individual</u> <u>savings</u> account. (In fact, this was true at the time. It just didn't stay that way for very long.)

Just like the lies told about the personal income tax (taxes would be a very small percentage and only paid by the rich), getting the people to accept new government programs (turn over personal power to the State) requires the deception that it will be either "painless (only affecting the other guy) or "in our own best interest".

Lie #2:

Your Social Security number is not to be used as identification. I still have my original card so I don't know if new cards have been changed but mine says very clearly in capital letters: "NOT FOR IDENTIFCATION". Again, true at the time, but government is first and foremost about force. Nothing the government touts as voluntary ever stays that way for long. Try to get a job without your **voluntary** Social Security number today.

Lie # 3, The biggest lie of all.

The Social Security Trust Fund would be **segregated** from other government funds. This also was true until the politicians realized what a "windfall" these funds were for their government expansion plans.

Today there is nothing in this so-called segregated "trust fund" except IOUs. The money has been siphoned off and used as general expense funds for whatever bureaucratic waste (or wealth redistribution) the politicians decided was in **their best interest**.

The Real Tragedy of Social Security

I disagree with those who consider Social Security to be just another form of welfare (it's actually become just another tax scheme). I was there from nearly the beginning. Social Security as proposed and enacted was one of the few good ideas to come out of the "New Deal".

The money we put into each of our **individual accounts** on a voluntary basis was to be invested on our behalf. At retirement we would receive time-payments based on whatever our accounts were worth, similar to an annuity.

So, in my opinion, confusing the Social Security fraud by calling it welfare misses the point completely. **The point again is that politicians cannot be trusted with our money**. Even a good idea under the control of government politicians will be corrupted and misused to the point of our own capital destruction.

It could be argued that the period from the end of WWII to the turn of this century was our most productive in history. **If the capital of those who had paid into Social Security from their own production,** had actually been invested in US Treasuries let alone the private sector, the Social Security Trust Fund would have been enormous.

Again, we can thank the infinite stupidity and greed for power of our so-called political leaders. **This vast potential growth of capital and wealth has been stolen from us and squandered on more wealth redistribution schemes to benefit an ever-growing government.**

We can't even blame the central bankers for this one. Yes, they have destroyed the buying power of our money, so that Social Security payments buy less and less, but it was our government politicians who stole (ongoing) our Social Security Trust Fund.

What the political collective did to Social Security, it did to every aspect of our American potential prosperity. It used to take just one income to support our families now it takes two or more to maintain the same standard of living that our parents or grandparents enjoyed.

We are becoming poorer, less efficient, less competent, less charitable, less healthy, **and less productive**; a nation of followers. **With few exceptions, we have no true leaders, only political sycophants and prima donnas; Parasites controlled by an inner circle of Vampires.**

Now the government wants to nationalize more of our Tier 1 necessary consumption items by controlling our health care (universal health care) and our energy with so-called "Green Initiatives" like "Cap and Trade" (just more special interest groups usurping government force for economic control).

The vampires want to take over more of our private industries all in the name of "protecting our economy" (or our environment) and doing "what's best for us". Please!!!

Just remember how government has handled Social Security and tell me you still think giving more control over our society and economy to government parasites is a good idea! It's time to Wake Up!

In Conclusion:

The elitist central planners in government, banking, business and other special interest groups are the Vampires and Parasites turning our country into a nation of Cannibals living off the economic bodies of our neighbors.

Humans are the only beings on this planet (as far as I know) with the mental capacity to <u>consciously</u> understand the relatively simple concepts of economics. Anyone who fails to use this capacity is no better than the domesticated animals in the field and will suffer the same fate.

The political, academic, banking and industrial elite would like nothing better than for you to ignore these issues. I know (or at least hope) you are smarter than that.

The battle for our individual economic and personal freedom and our very survival as a civilized free nation is at stake and nearly lost.

World Government Fascism / Socialism or Individual and Economic Freedom; which side are you taking?

For more information on all aspects of economics and individual freedom, check out these websites:

www.mises.org   www.lewrockwell.com

www.campaignforliberty.com   www.yaliberty.org

www.downsizedc.org   www.losthorizons.com

CPSIA information can be obtained at www.ICGtesting.com
Printed in the USA
LVOW08s2108310315

432755LV00022B/462/P